LET'S LEARN ABOUT...
THE OCEAN

PROJECT BOOK

PRE-CODING

K1

Pearson

Pearson Education Limited
KAO Two, KAO Park, Harlow, Essex, CM17 9NA, England
and Associated Companies around the world

First published 2020

ISBN: 978-1-292-33409-7

Set in Mundo Sans
Printed in China SWTC/01

Acknowledgements
The publishers and author(s) would like to thank the following people and institutions for their feedback and comments during the development of the material: Marcos Mendonça, Leandra Dias, Viviane Kirmeliene, Rhiannon Ball, Simara H. Dal'Alba, Mônica Bicalho and GB Editorial. The publishers would also like to thank all the teachers who contributed to the development of *Let's learn about…*: Adriano de Paula Souza, Aline Ramos Teixeira Santo, Aline Vitor Rodrigues Pina Pereira, Ana Paula Gomez Montero, Anna Flávia Feitosa Passos, Camila Jarola, Celiane Junker Silva, Edegar França Junior, Fabiana Reis Yoshio, Fernanda de Souza Thomaz, Luana da Silva, Michael Iacovino Luidvinavicius, Munique Dias de Melo, Priscila Rossatti Duval Ferreira Neves, Sandra Ferito, and schools that took part in Construindo Juntos.

Author Acknowledgements
Luciana Pinheiro, Rhiannon Ball

Illustration Acknowledgements
Illustrated by Filipe Laurentino and Silva Serviços de Educação

Cover illustration © Filipe Laurentino

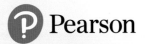

CONTENTS

ROLL AND COLOR.

  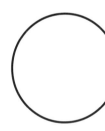

LISTEN AND STICK. SING.

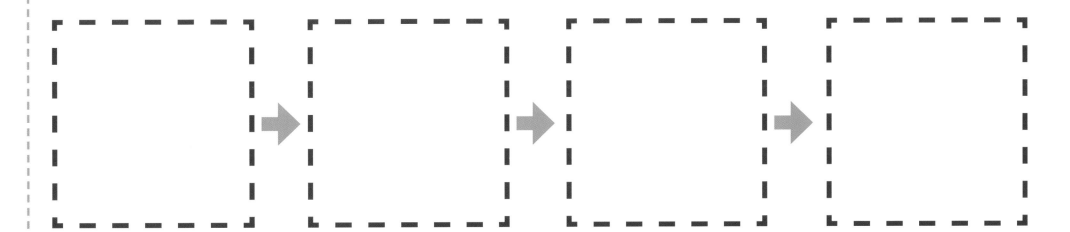

DRAW AND COLOR. SAY.

COLOR. SAY AND DO.

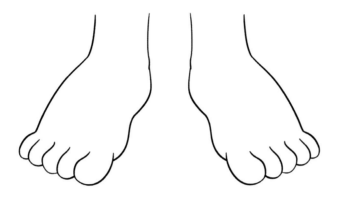

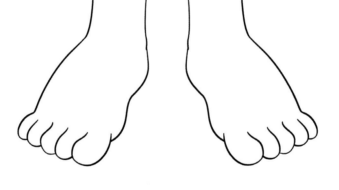

⬤	**1**
⬤	**2**
⬤	**3**
⬤	**4**

COUNT AND CROSS OUT. SAY. **X**

 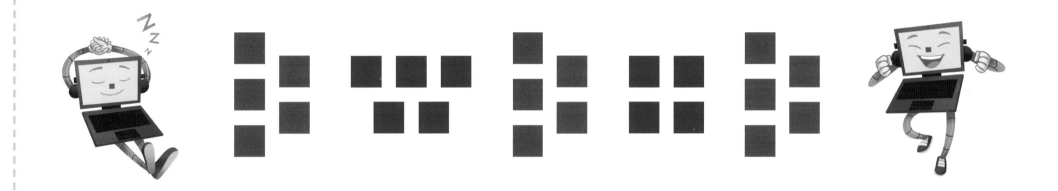 

LOOK AND STICK.

LOOK AND COUNT. COLOR.

ROLL AND DRAW AN X. STICK.

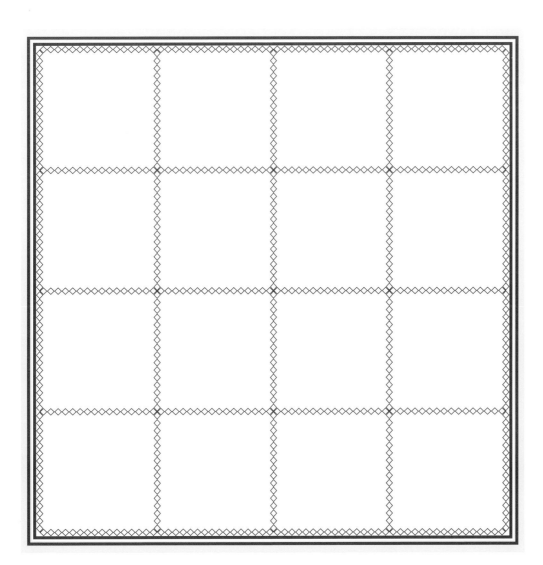

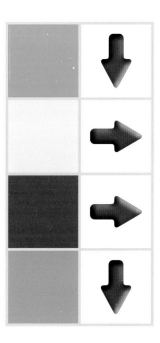

LOOK AND COLOR. THEN CIRCLE.

START

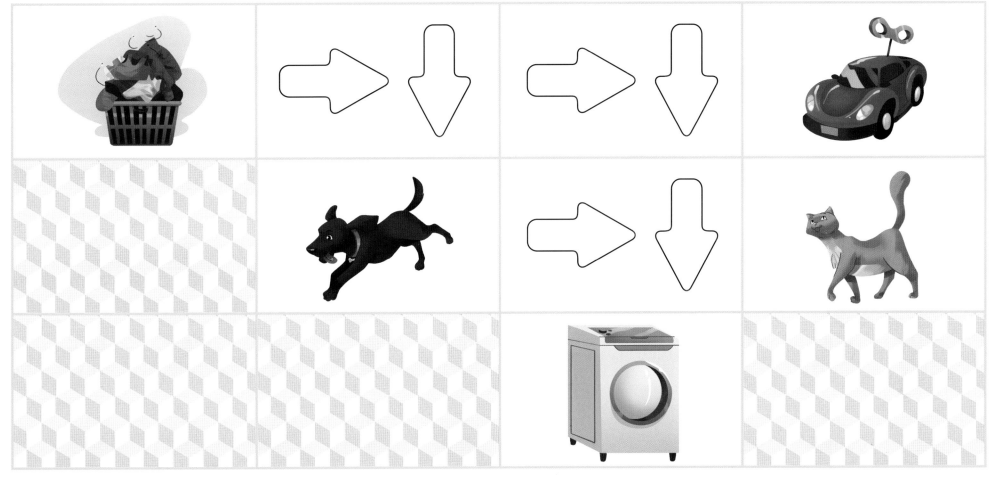

FINISH

 1

 2

 3

COUNT AND COLOR.  3

LOOK AND MATCH.

LOOK AND CROSS OUT.

HELP THE BEAR GET TO THE HONEY.

LOOK, COLOR, AND DRAW.

STICK. TELL YOUR CLASSMATE.

OCEAN OCEAN OCEAN OCEAN OCEAN OCEAN OCEAN
OCEAN OCEAN OCEAN OCEAN OCEAN OCEAN
OCEAN OCEAN OCEAN OCEAN OCEAN OCEAN
OCEAN OCEAN OCEAN OCEAN OCEAN OCEAN
OCEAN OCEAN OCEAN OCEAN OCEAN OCEAN

LOOK AND COLOR.

DRAW.

DRAW.

DRAW.

DRAW.

OCEAN OCEAN OCEAN OCEAN OCEAN OCEAN
OCEAN OCEAN OCEAN OCEAN OCEAN OCEAN
OCEAN OCEAN OCEAN OCEAN OCEAN OCEAN
OCEAN OCEAN OCEAN OCEAN OCEAN OCEAN

DRAW.

STICKERS